ONE THOUSAND THINGS

WIDE EYED EDITIONS

CONTENTS

Can you spot me in every scene?

FIRST

things to learn

DO YOU KNOW YOUR COLOURS?

pink

red

purple

brown

yellow

light blue

blue

olive green

dark blue

orange

grey

green

rose

7

CAN YOU COUNT
FROM ONE TO TEN?

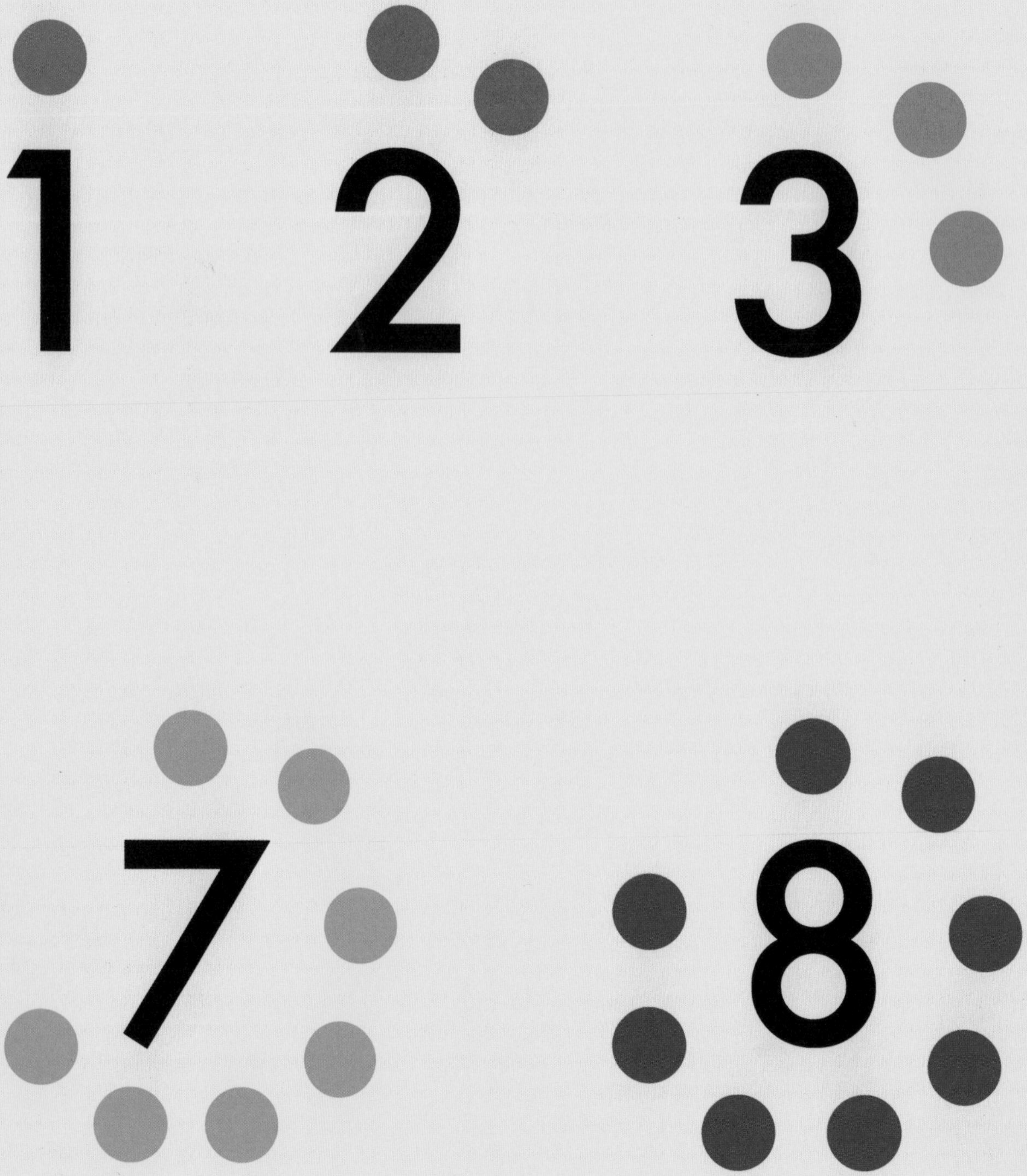

1

2

3

7

8

4   5   6

9   10

WHAT ARE THESE
DIFFERENT SHAPES?

heart

circle

diamond

star

triangle

rectangle

square

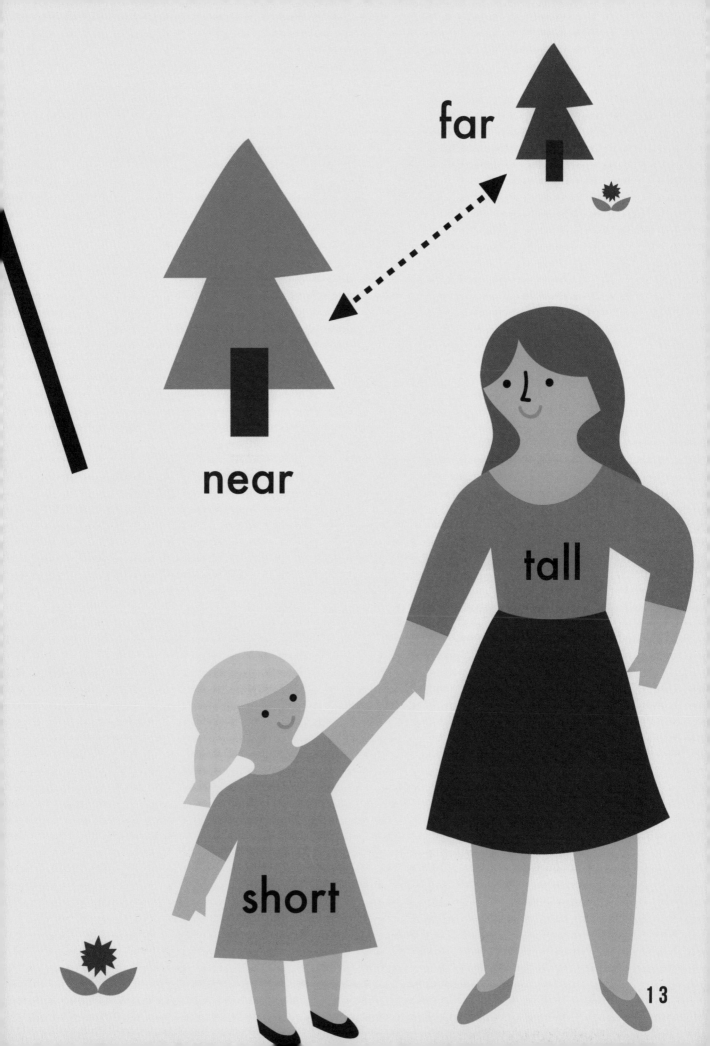

far

near

tall

short

13

WHAT ARE THE DIFFERENT TIMES OF DAY?

morning

night

14

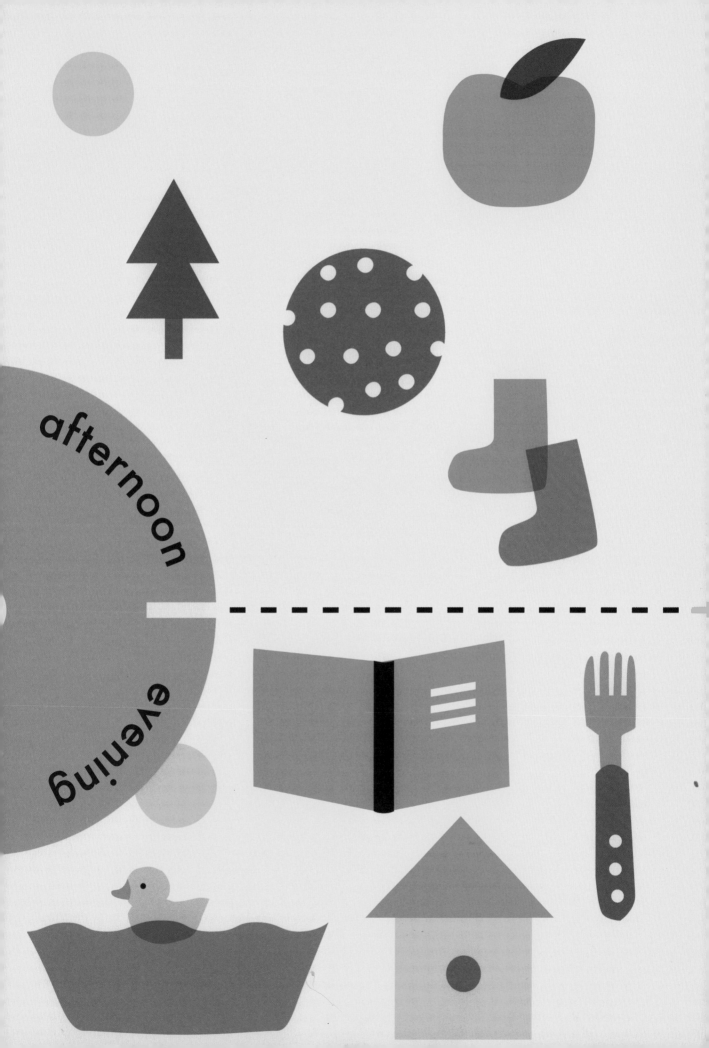

afternoon

evening

THINGS

to do with you →

WHAT ARE THE PARTS OF YOUR FACE CALLED?

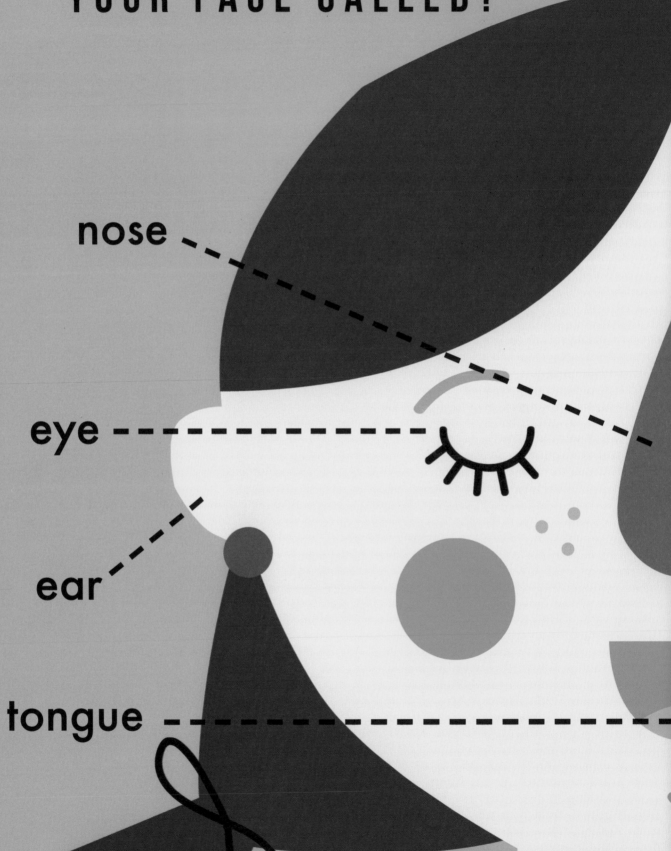

nose

eye

ear

tongue

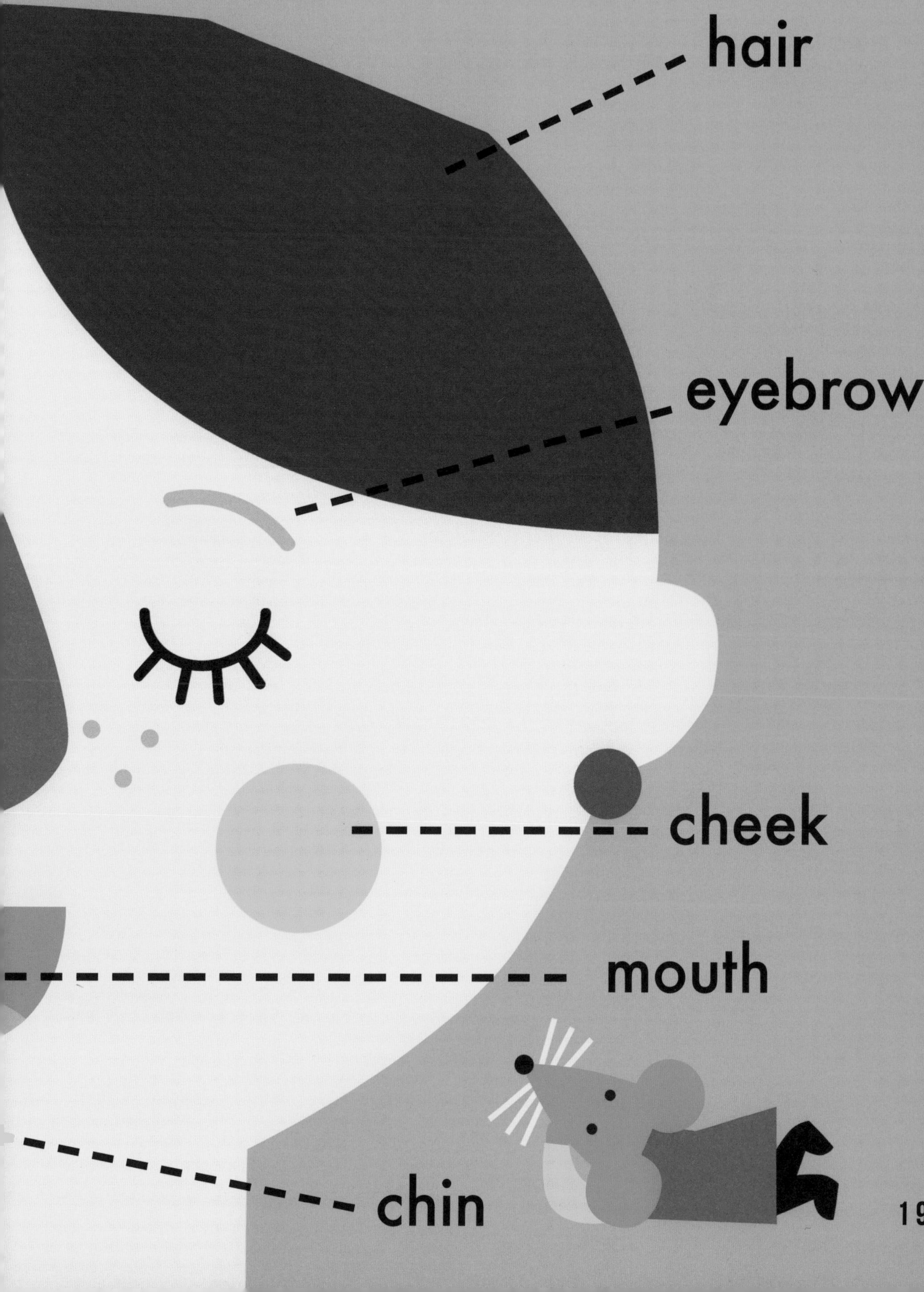

hair

eyebrow

cheek

mouth

chin

WHAT ARE YOUR FIVE SENSES?

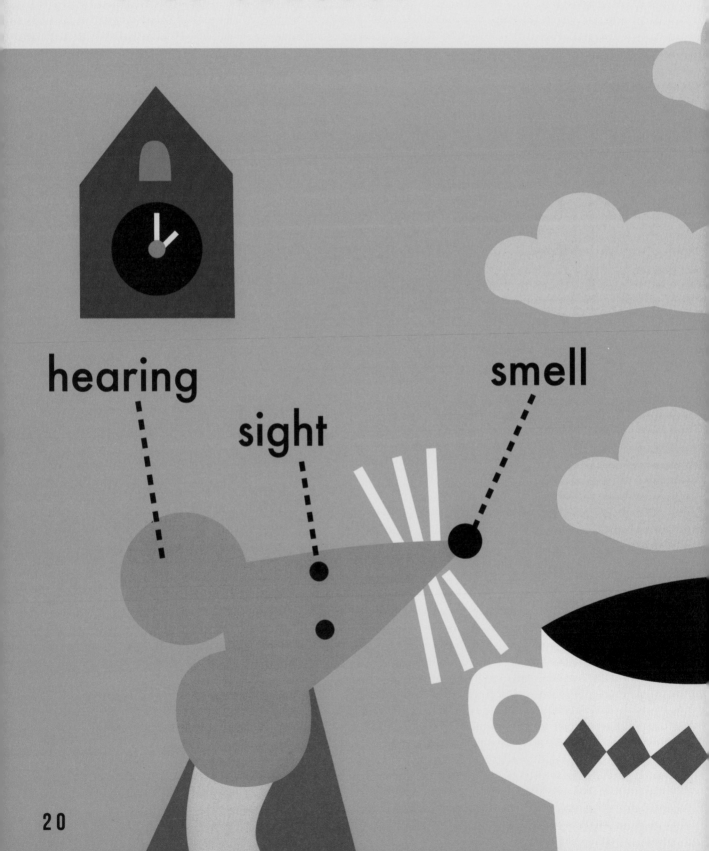

hearing

sight

smell

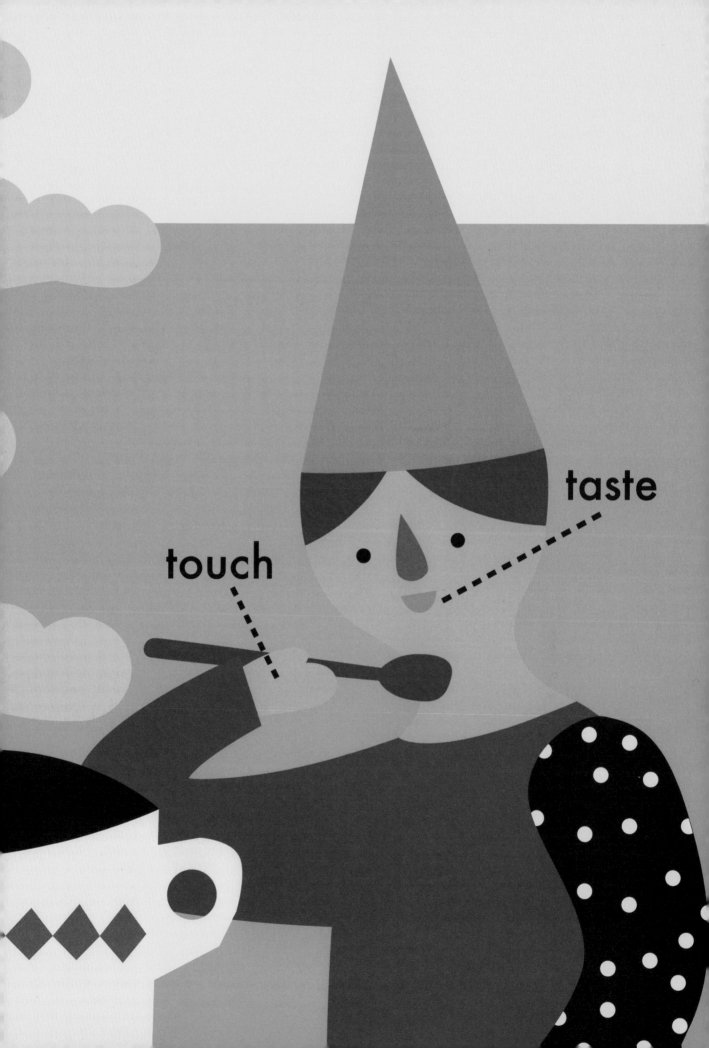

WHAT ARE THE DIFFERENT PARTS OF YOUR BODY?

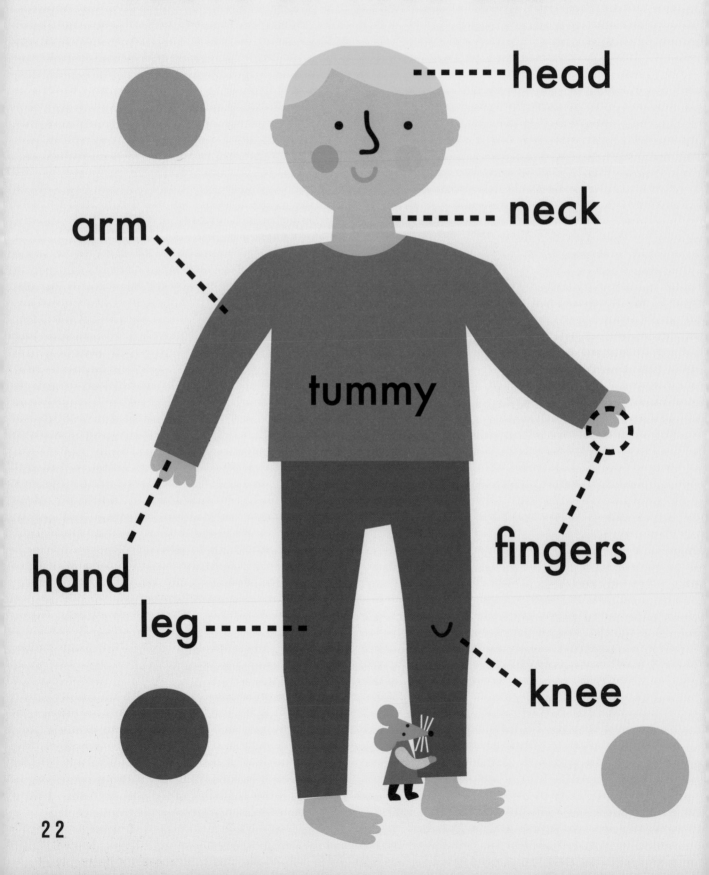

head

neck

arm

tummy

fingers

hand

leg

knee

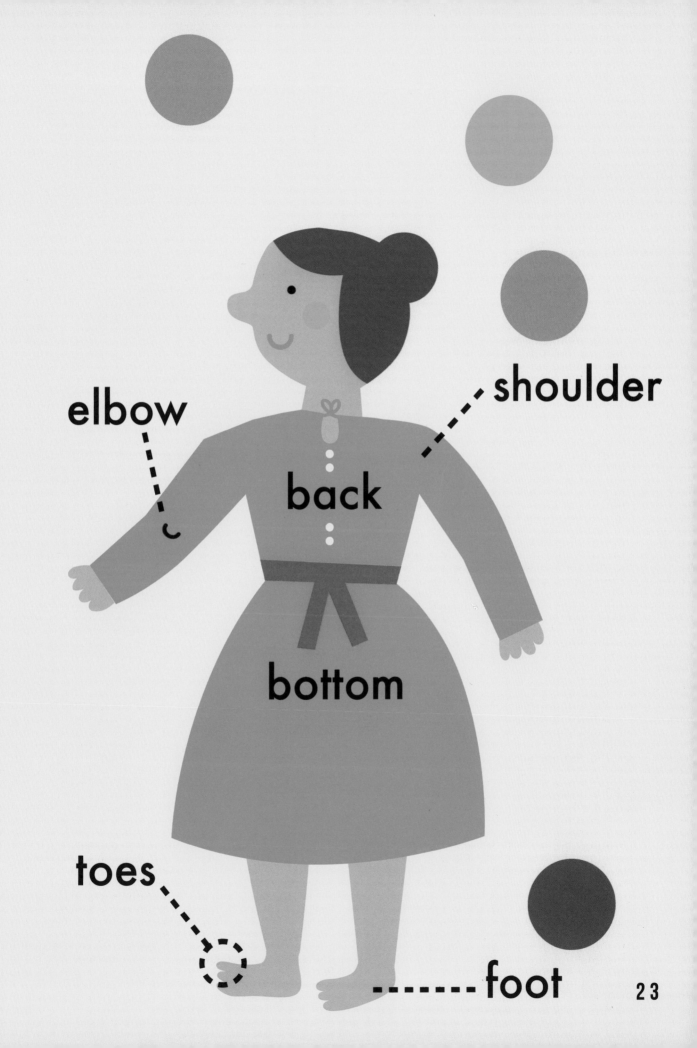

elbow

shoulder

back

bottom

toes

foot

23

WHAT WOULD YOU LIKE TO WEAR TODAY?

trousers

jumper

dress

pyjamas

top

glove

hat

underpants

coat

socks

shirt

shoes

25

WHO IS IN YOUR FAMILY?

cousin

dad

mum

sister

aunty

uncle

grandpa

granny

brother

THINGS
around the world

WHAT ARE THE FOUR SEASONS?

spring

autumn

summer

winter

WHAT WEATHER DO WE HAVE TODAY?

wind

sun

thunder
and
lightning

rain

rainbow

WHAT CAN YOU FIND IN SPACE?

sun

moon

rocket - - - - - -

planet

star ----- •

----- astronaut

THINGS

in nature

WHAT'S IN THE FRUIT BOWL?

cherry

pear

plum

apple

watermelon

mango

WHAT VEGETABLES CAN YOU SEE?

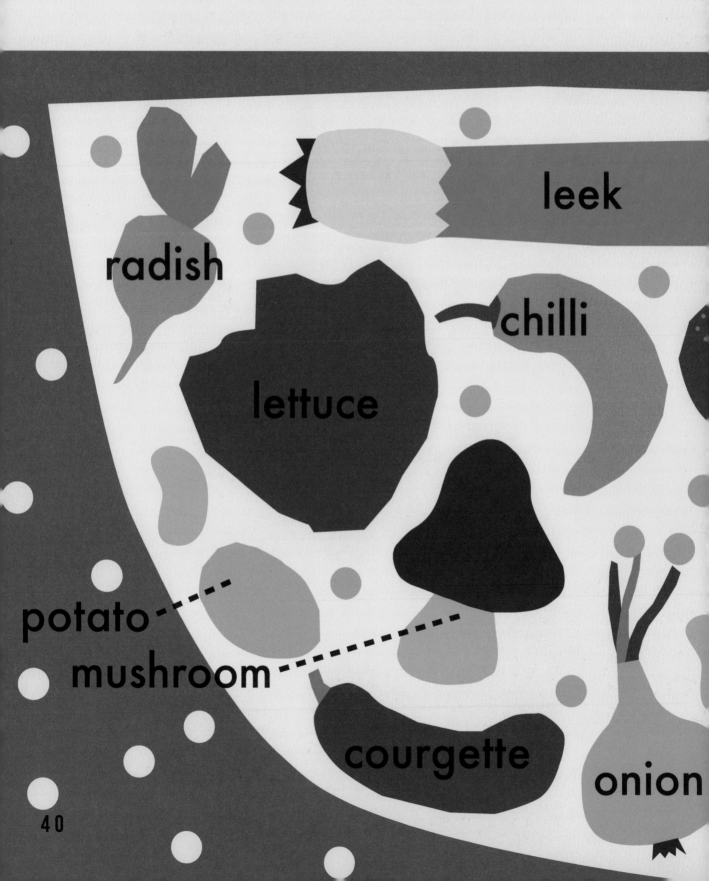

leek

radish

chilli

lettuce

potato

mushroom

courgette

onion

tomato

garlic

broccoli

cabbage

cauliflower

WHAT ANIMALS LIVE ON THE FARM?

cow

butterfly

hen

dog

sheep

bee

goat

horse

duck

pig

WHAT ANIMALS LIVE IN THE WILD?

spider

rhinoceros

parrot

lion

crocodile

snake

giraffe

monkey

elephant

tiger

zebra

45

WHAT ANIMALS LIVE IN THE SEA?

octopus

fish

shark

dolphin

whale

seahorse

crab

starfish

WHAT ANIMALS WOULD YOU HAVE FOUND LONG AGO?

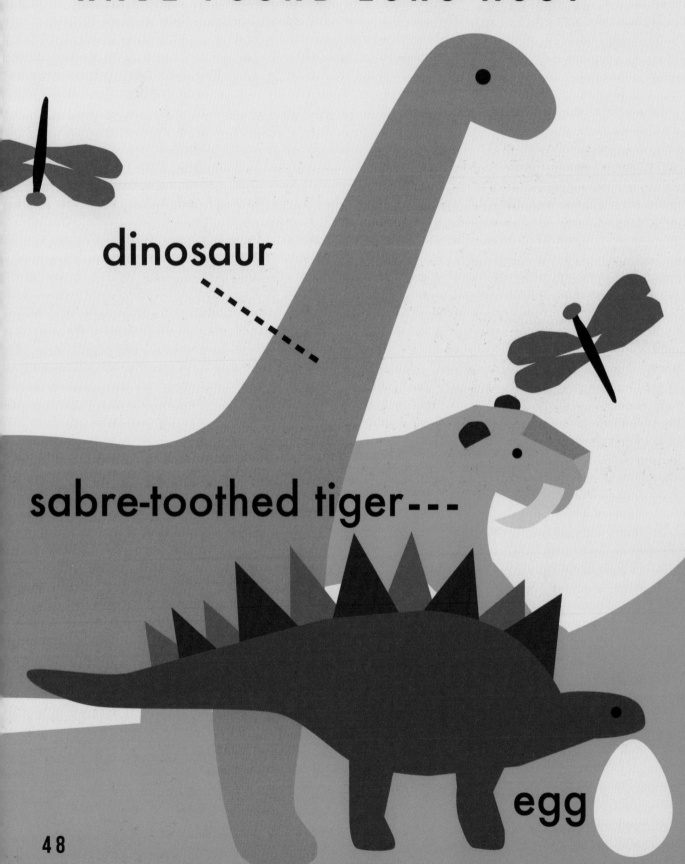

dinosaur

sabre-toothed tiger ---

egg

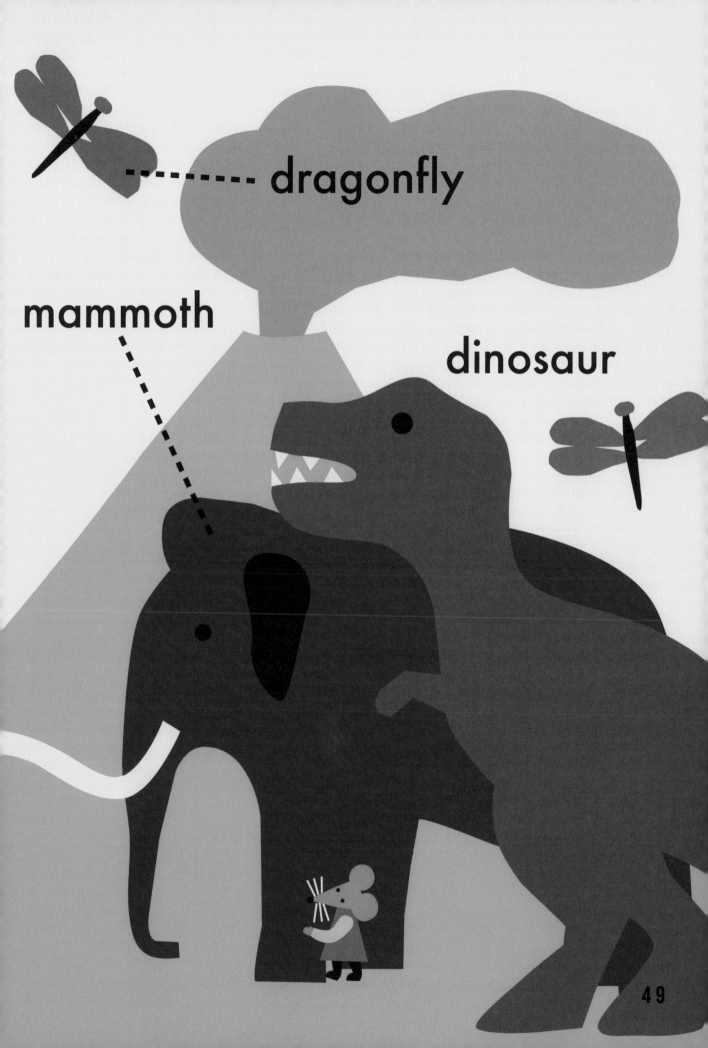

dragonfly

mammoth

dinosaur

THINGS

that you can do

WHAT CAN YOU DO OUTSIDE?

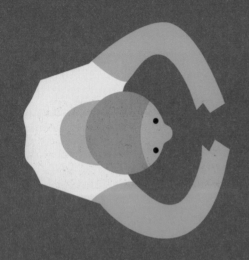

swim

kick

dance

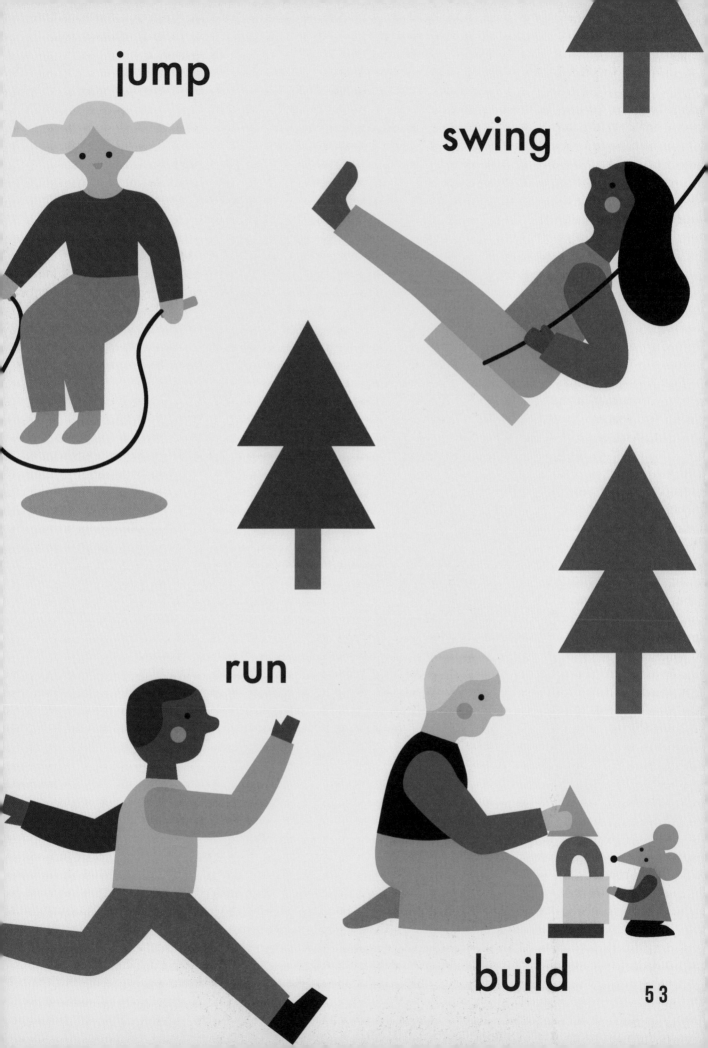

jump

swing

run

build

53

WHAT CAN YOU DO INSIDE?

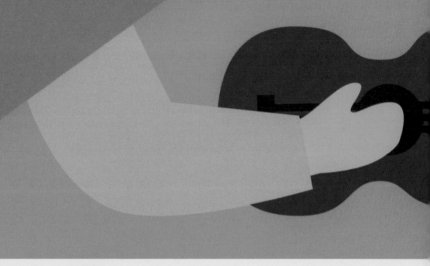

read

play

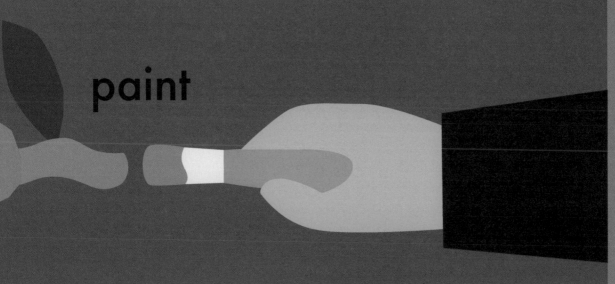

paint

write

WHAT DO YOU DO EVERY DAY?

eat

laugh

wash

share

hug

sleep

57

WHAT WILL YOU BE WHEN YOU GROW UP?

artist

builder

chef

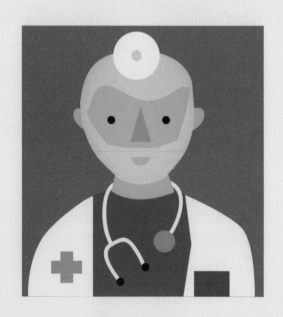

doctor

farmer

musician

teacher

vet

THINGS

inside your house

WHAT CAN YOU SEE IN THE KITCHEN?

cup

saucepan

oven

fork

plate

knife

teapot

fridge

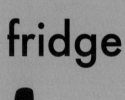

spoon

bowl

WHAT CAN YOU FIND IN THE BATHROOM?

towel

shower

sponge

bath

soap

toothbrush

toilet

WHAT CAN YOU SEE IN THE BEDROOM?

books

clock

night light

teddy

pillow

bed

toys

chair

wardrobe

WHAT CAN YOU FIND IN THE SHED?

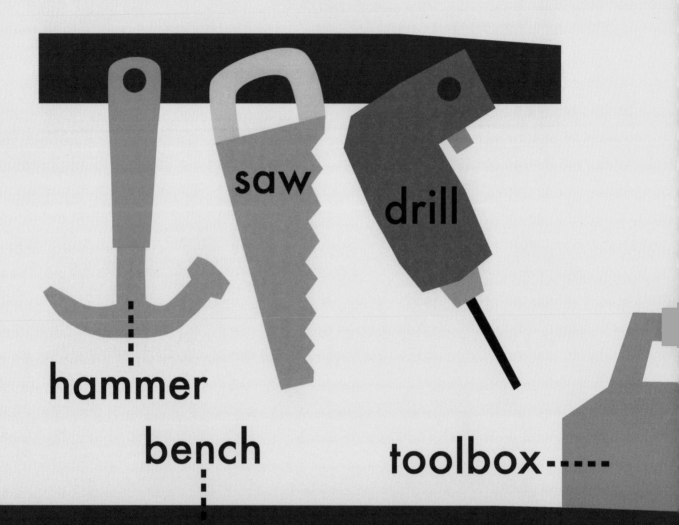

saw

drill

hammer

bench

toolbox-----

----- boots

spanner

screwdriver

nails

ladder

THINGS

outside your house

WHAT ARE THESE THINGS THAT GO?

tractor

car

boat

plane

bicycle

fire engine

73

WHAT ARE THESE BUILDINGS CALLED?

castle

tower

barn

school

house

bridge

WHAT CAN YOU FIND IN NATURE?

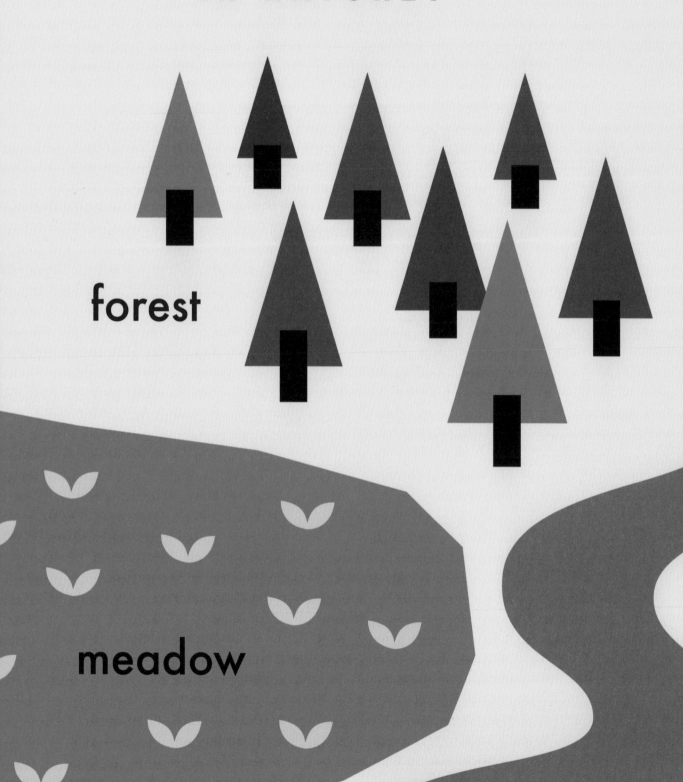

forest

meadow

river

mountain

tree

lake

SO, WHAT DOES 1,000...

REALLY LOOK LIKE?

Wide Eyed Editions
www.wideeyededitions.com

One Thousand Things copyright © Aurum Press Ltd 2015
Illustrations copyright © Anna Kövecses 2015

First published in Great Britain in 2015 by
Wide Eyed Editions, an imprint of Aurum Press,
74–77 White Lion Street, London N1 9PF
www.aurumpress.co.uk

A catalogue record for this book is available from the British Library.

ISBN 978-1-84780-607-9

The illustrations were created digitally
Set in Fugue, Bebas Neue and Futura Medium

Designed by Andrew Watson
Edited by Jenny Broom

Printed in Dongguan, Guangdong, China

1 3 5 7 9 8 6 4 2